Creating and
Selling Digital
Products

Creating and Selling Digital Products

The Comprehensive Guide

Ash Layna

Introduction

Our world is undergoing a digital revolution. A revolution fueled by innovation, technology, and the limitless possibilities of the digital realm. Today, the landscape of commerce, communication, and creation has been dramatically reshaped, and central to this transformation is the rise of digital products.

The term 'digital products' encompasses a wide variety of items - anything that is created, distributed, and consumed in an electronic format. This includes eBooks, music, films, software, apps, online courses, graphics, web-based services, and many more. Unlike physical goods, these products are not bound by material, logistics, or traditional manufacturing constraints.

They can be created once and sold endlessly without the need for restocking or shipping, making them an attractive proposition for entrepreneurs and creatives alike.

Digital products emerged as a niche market with the advent of the internet but have since proliferated into the mainstream. In recent years, the expansion of global connectivity, the proliferation of devices, and changing consumer behaviors have driven the unprecedented growth of digital products. From the world's largest tech companies down to individual creatives in their home studios, digital products have become an integral part of our economy.

This rise of digital products isn't just a trend – it's an evolution of the way we create, sell, and consume. They have made it possible for anyone with a skill, a passion, or a unique idea to reach an audience and generate an income.

The potential of creating and selling digital products is immense. Whether you're an established business looking to diversify your offerings, a start-up aiming to disrupt the market, or an individual yearning to turn your creativity into a revenue stream, digital products offer unique opportunities.

Creating and selling digital products can offer a number of benefits, such as the abil ity to work from anywhere, the freedom to be your own boss, scalability, low start-up costs, and the chance to earn passive income. In addition, digital products can also be a powerful tool for building a personal brand or business, reaching a global audience, and making a positive impact in your chosen field.

However, like any venture, it's not without challenges. The journey from idea to product to profit involves various stages of planning, designing, creating, testing, launching, marketing, and customer engagement. Each of these stages requires knowledge, skills, tools, and strategies, which we aim to explore in this comprehensive guide.

This book, "Creating and Selling Digital Products: The Comprehensive Guide," is designed to help you navigate this exciting digital landscape. With step-by-step guides, insights, and

practical advice, we will guide you through the process of turning your digital product ideas into reality and, ultimately, profits.

Welcome to your journey in the world of digital products!

In the chapters that follow, we will delve into every aspect of creating and selling digital products. From idea generation, product development, and testing to launching, marketing, and customer relationship building, this book is your roadmap to launching your digital product business.

Chapter 1: Understanding Digital Products

What are Digital Products?

At the core of the digital revolution lie digital products. But what exactly are they? Simply put, digital products are goods that are produced, delivered, and consumed in an electronic or digital format. They are intangible and do not take up any physical space. Once created, they can be reproduced indefinitely without any additional production costs. Unlike physical products, digital products are not subject to wear and tear, do not require physical storage, and can be delivered to the customer instantly, no matter where in the world they are.

Types of Digital Products

The beauty of digital products lies in their vast variety and versatility. From knowledge-based products to entertainment, utility, and artistic expression, the scope of what can be digitized is virtually boundless.

One of the most common types of digital products is eBooks. These are digital versions of traditional books, from novels to instructional guides, that can be read on a variety of devices.

With the proliferation of e-readers and smartphones, eBooks have become increasingly popular and accessible to readers worldwide.

Another major category is online courses. These educational content offerings are delivered over the internet and can include video lectures, written content, interactive quizzes, and more.

As distance learning gains traction, online courses have become an essential tool for knowledge-sharing and skill-building.

Software and apps represent a massive segment of digital products. These programs, designed to perform specific tasks on a computer or mobile device, encompass everything from productivity tools to games. The ubiquity of mobile devices and the reliance on software across various industries make this an ever-growing category.

Digital products also encompass the realm of music and audio. Digital audio files include music tracks, audiobooks, podcasts, and sound effects. With the decline of physical media, digital distribution has become the primary method for delivering and consuming audio content.

In the field of digital art and design, creators offer graphics, logos, website templates, fonts, and other digital artistic creations. As visual content continues to dominate digital media, the demand for high-quality digital art and design is on the rise.

Photography also plays a significant role in the digital products space. High-resolution digital photos can be used for various purposes, from website design to advertising, making them a valuable asset for businesses and individuals alike.

Web-based services, such as cloud storage, SEO services, software as a service (SaaS), and more, are also considered digital products. As the internet continues to expand and integrate into our daily lives, web-based services have become essential components of the digital landscape.

Additionally, digital products can include videos, ranging from short films, documentaries, tutorials, animations, to stock footage. Videos have become one of the most consumed types of content online, and as such, a potentially lucrative digital product for creators.

Finally, with advancements in technology, virtual reality (VR) and augmented reality (AR) experiences represent the cutting edge of digital product design. As these technologies mature, they are likely to form a new and innovative category of digital products.

Benefits of Creating and Selling Digital Products

Digital products offer a variety of benefits over traditional physical goods, making them an attractive option for entrepreneurs and creatives alike.

First and foremost, digital products are highly scalable. Once a digital product is created, it can be sold an infinite number of times without any additional production or distribution costs. This scalability is one of the key attractions of digital products, as it allows for significant profit margins and growth potential.

Digital products also provide accessibility to a global market. Since they can be sold and delivered to customers anywhere in the world, creators are not limited by geographic boundaries. This global reach presents an enormous opportunity to tap

Chapter 2: Idea Generation for Digital Products Importance of Idea Generation

Idea generation is the critical first step in the creation of digital products. Without a compelling, unique, and valuable idea, the subsequent steps of design, development, and marketing fall flat. An idea forms the seed of your product, the blueprint upon which all else will be built.

Furthermore, it's not merely about having an idea, but having the right idea—one that aligns with your skills, interests, and the market demand. Therefore, the importance of dedicating thoughtful time and effort into idea generation cannot be overstated.

Methods for Generating Ideas

Generating a profitable idea for a digital product requires creativity, research, and sometimes, a bit of serendipity. Fortunately, there are numerous methods to stimulate the idea generation process:

1. **Examine Your Skills and Passions:** Start by taking inventory of your skills, expertise, and passions. Is there a subject you're particularly knowledgeable about or a skill you excel in? Digital

products often succeed when the creator is passionate and knowledgeable about the topic.

2. **Identify Market Needs:** Research your chosen industry or niche to identify any gaps or unmet needs. What are people struggling with? What solutions are they seeking?

Engage in forums, read industry blogs, or survey your target market to gather insights.

3. **Leverage Trends:** Keep an eye on emerging trends and technological advancements. Can you leverage a new trend or technology to create a cutting-edge digital product?

4. **Solve a Problem:** People often buy products to solve a problem. Think about problems you've encountered and consider if a digital product could offer a solution.

5. **Brainstorm:** Use traditional brainstorming techniques, either alone or in a group, to generate a list of potential ideas. Don't dismiss any idea at this stage; even the most outlandish thoughts could evolve into a viable product.

Identifying the Target Market

Once you've generated a pool of ideas, it's crucial to identify who your target market is. Who are the potential buyers of your digital product? Your target market should be a specific group of people who share a common need that your product addresses. The better you understand your target market, the more effectively you can design, develop, and market your product to meet their specific needs and preferences.

Consider factors such as age, gender, occupation, interests, challenges, and buying behaviors when identifying your target market. Remember, trying to appeal to everyone often results in appealing to no one. By having a clear target market, you can focus your efforts and tailor your product to match their specific requirements.

Evaluating the Feasibility of Your Idea Not all ideas are feasible or profitable. Once you have an idea and have identified a potential target market, it's time to evaluate the feasibility of your idea. This involves assessing whether you can realistically create the product and whether there's a viable market for it.

Questions to ask during this evaluation process may include: 6. **Do I have the skills and resources to create this product?** If not, can I acquire them or outsource the necessary tasks?

7. **Is there a demand for this product?** Use market research tools, check competitor offerings, and engage with your target market to validate demand.

8. **Can I sell this product at a price that is profitable yet affordable for my target market?**

This requires an estimation of the cost to develop and market the product and an understanding of the price your target market is willing to pay.

9. **Can I reach my target market effectively?** Consider how you'll market your product and whether you can reach your target market through these channels.

By the end of this evaluation process, you should have a clear understanding of the feasibility of your digital product idea. It's okay if your initial idea doesn't pass this feasibility test. Use the insights gained during this process to refine your idea or generate new ones. Remember, the journey to a profitable digital product often involves exploration, experimentation, and even a few wrong turns along the way.

Chapter 3: Product Design and Development

Designing Digital Products: Essential Elements When it comes to digital product design, the process transcends the visual aesthetics; it involves shaping the user experience, functionality, and overall usability of the product. These elements are crucial in determining whether a digital product engages the user or gets abandoned halfway through use.

Designing a digital product begins with a solid understanding of the product's core purpose.

This purpose will guide your design choices and help ensure your product delivers its intended value. Each element of your product should support this core purpose.

Usability is another vital element in digital product design. A product could be visually stunning, but if it's hard to navigate or doesn't function as expected, users will quickly abandon it.

Therefore, it's crucial to prioritize the user experience in your design process. Strive for simplicity and intuitiveness in your design. The goal is to make the user's interaction with your product as seamless and effortless as possible.

The aesthetic of your digital product also plays an important role. This includes color schemes, typography, imagery, and layout. A well-designed product not only draws the user in but also enhances the user's interaction with the product. Aesthetics should complement functionality, creating a visually appealing product that's also user-friendly.

Best Practices in Digital Product Design

Designing a successful digital product is both an art and a science. Here are some key best practices to keep in mind throughout the design process: Firstly, keep your user at the forefront of your design process. This user-centric design approach involves understanding your user's needs, preferences, and behaviors and incorporating this understanding into your design. Engage your users in the design process through user testing and feedback.

Secondly, consistency is key in digital product design. Ensure consistency in your design elements such as colors, typography, and navigational elements across your product.

Consistency enhances usability and helps build a sense of familiarity and trust with your users.

Additionally, focus on simplicity. A cluttered or overly complicated design can overwhelm users and detract from the product's core functionality. Stick to the essentials and remove any unnecessary elements that don't contribute to the product's purpose or user experience.

Lastly, remember that design is an iterative process. Don't be afraid to experiment, make mistakes, and learn from them. Continually testing and refining your design based on user feedback and performance metrics can lead to a better final product.

Prototyping Your Digital Product

Before moving into full-fledged product development, creating a prototype can be an invaluable step. A prototype is a preliminary version of your product that allows you to visualize the design, test the functionality, and gather feedback.

Prototyping helps you identify potential issues and areas of improvement before investing significant time and resources into development. It can also serve as a useful tool for communicating your product concept to potential investors, collaborators, or users.

Tools and Resources for Digital Product Development The digital era has brought forth an array of tools and resources to aid in digital product development. While the specific tools will depend on the type of digital product you're creating, there are several categories of tools you might need.

For graphic design and visual elements, tools like Adobe Creative Suite or Canva can be invaluable. For developing websites or apps, coding platforms and frameworks such as Visual Studio Code, React, or Swift might come in handy. If you're creating an eBook or online course, you might need content creation tools like Google Docs, PowerPoint, or e-learning platforms like Teachable or Thinkific.

Moreover, for prototyping, tools like Sketch, Adobe XD, or Figma offer robust functionalities for creating interactive prototypes. For project management and collaboration, tools like Asana, Trello, or Slack can help keep your development process organized and streamlined.

Choosing the right tools can increase your efficiency and enable you to create a higher quality product. Therefore, it's worth investing time in exploring different tools, their capabilities, and how they can support your product development process.

Chapter 4: Step-by-step Guide to Creating an eBook
Understanding the eBook Landscape

As we delve into the world of eBook creation, let's first establish an understanding of what an eBook is. An eBook, or electronic book, is a book that is available in digital format. It can be read on various devices, such as e-readers, tablets, smartphones, and computers. The great advantage of eBooks is their portability, accessibility, and the ease with which they can be distributed globally, transcending geographical boundaries.

The rise of self-publishing and the accessibility of eBook platforms have democratized the publishing industry, opening doors for independent authors and experts across all fields to share their knowledge and creativity with the world. So, whether you're an aspiring novelist, a professional aiming to share industry insights, or a hobbyist looking to turn your passion into a digital product, the eBook format offers immense potential.

Identifying Your Topic

Creating a successful eBook starts with a compelling topic. The best topics often lie at the intersection of your expertise, passions, and market demand. It's crucial that you feel enthusiastic about your chosen subject; this enthusiasm will keep you motivated throughout the writing process and will shine through in your writing, engaging your readers.

Your topic should also provide value to your readers. Whether it's teaching a new skill, providing insights, telling a captivating story, or addressing a common problem, your eBook should offer something of value that will entice readers to purchase and read it.

Researching and Outlining Your eBook

Once you have your topic, the next step is to conduct thorough research. This involves gathering information, facts, and ideas to include in your eBook. Even if you're well-versed in your topic, research can help you deepen your understanding, discover new perspectives, and ensure your information is up-to-date and accurate.

After you've completed your research, it's time to create an outline for your eBook. This will serve as your roadmap during the writing process. Start with the main sections or chapters of your eBook and then break each section down into smaller subtopics or key points. An outline helps you organize your thoughts, ensures you cover all necessary points, and keeps you on track while writing.

Writing Your eBook

With your outline in hand, you're ready to start writing. This is where your idea begins to come to life. Remember, writing is a process; it doesn't have to be perfect on the first try. The key is to start writing and keep the momentum going. Focus on one section at a time, and before you know it, you'll have a complete draft of your eBook.

As you write, keep your target audience in mind. Use a tone and language that resonates with them. Make your writing engaging and easy to understand. Break up your text into short paragraphs and use subheadings, bullet points, or lists to make your content easy to digest.

Editing and Formatting Your eBook

Once you have your draft, it's time to edit. Editing involves reviewing your content for clarity, coherence, grammar, and punctuation errors. It's often beneficial to take a break after writing and before editing, so you can review your work with fresh eyes. You may also consider hiring a professional editor or using editing software to help with this process.

Formatting is another crucial step in eBook creation. This involves arranging your content in a visually appealing and easy-to-read way. Consider aspects such as headers, footers, page numbers, table of contents, font style, font size, line spacing, and paragraph alignment. Most eBook publishing platforms require your eBook to be in a specific format (usually .epub or

.mobi), so ensure your formatting is compatible.

Designing Your eBook Cover

They say don't judge a book by its cover, but the truth is, a well-designed cover can significantly influence a potential reader's decision to purchase your eBook. Your cover should be visually appealing and convey the essence of your eBook. You can design your cover using graphic design tools, hire a professional designer, or use templates provided by eBook publishing platforms.

Publishing and Marketing Your eBook

Once your eBook is written, edited, formatted, and has a captivating cover, it's time to publish.

There are various platforms for eBook publishing, such as Amazon Kindle Direct Publishing, Smashwords, or Apple's iBooks, each with its own set of guidelines and processes. Choose the platform that best suits your needs and follow their steps for eBook submission.

Publishing your eBook is only half the battle; marketing is the key to reaching your readers. Use social media, email marketing, content marketing, and other promotional strategies to create awareness about your eBook, generate interest, and drive sales. Remember to target your marketing efforts towards your identified target audience.

Conclusion

Creating an eBook can be a rewarding experience, allowing you to share your knowledge, express your creativity, establish your authority, and generate income. While the process requires effort, dedication, and patience, the potential benefits make it a worthwhile endeavor.

So get your ideas flowing, and start your eBook creation journey today!

Chapter 5: Step-by-step Guide to Creating Online Courses
The Rise of Online Learning

As digital technology continues to reshape our lives, the landscape of education and learning has been one of its most significant arenas of change. Today, knowledge is no longer confined to the four walls of traditional classrooms; it is available anytime, anywhere, at the click of a button. Online courses, in particular, have emerged as a popular form of learning, offering flexibility, accessibility, and a wide range of topics.

Creating an online course is a compelling way to share your expertise, engage with learners worldwide, and generate income. Whether you're a professional looking to teach industry-specific skills, a hobbyist sharing your passion, or an entrepreneur teaching business strategies, the possibilities are endless.

Choosing Your Course Topic

Just like eBooks, choosing a topic for your online course involves identifying an area where your expertise or passion aligns with a demand in the market. Your course should offer valuable knowledge or skills that your target audience wants to learn.

When selecting your course topic, consider your strengths, what you enjoy, and what you feel confident teaching. It's also important to research and understand your potential learners'

needs and desires. What are they interested in learning? What problems do they need solutions for?

Planning Your Course

Once you've chosen a topic, the next step is to plan your course. Start by defining the objectives of your course. What will students learn by the end of the course? What skills or knowledge will they acquire?

Then, structure your course content. Break down your course into manageable modules or sections, each focusing on a specific topic or concept. Within each module, create individual lessons. This modular structure helps organize your content, makes it easier for students to follow along, and allows them to progress at their own pace.

Creating Your Course Content

Creating content for your online course involves a combination of writing, filming, and possibly, audio recording.

For the written content, like course descriptions, lesson outlines, and quizzes, make sure your language is clear, concise, and engaging.

Most online courses include video content. Filming your course requires a bit more technical setup, including a good quality camera, a microphone, and proper lighting. Remember to present yourself in a professional and engaging manner.

Additionally, creating high-quality slides or visual aids to accompany your teachings can significantly enhance your course.

Remember, the key to effective teaching is not just to provide information but to make learning engaging and interactive. Consider integrating quizzes, assignments, and discussion forums into your course.

Editing and Uploading Your Course

After creating your course content, review and edit it carefully to ensure it is polished, professional, and free of errors. If your course includes video content, you may need to use video editing software.

Once your content is ready, it's time to upload it to an online course platform. There are several platforms available, each with its own features and pricing structures, such as Udemy, Coursera, or Teachable. Select the platform that best fits your needs and upload your course following their specific guidelines.

Promoting Your Course

Once your course is live, the final step is to promote it. Similar to marketing an eBook, effective promotion strategies can include social media marketing, content marketing, email marketing, and more.

Remember, successful promotion is not just about reaching a wide audience, but about reaching the right audience—those who are most likely to be interested in your course topic.

In Summary

Creating an online course can be a rewarding endeavor, allowing you to share your knowledge, engage with learners worldwide, and generate income. Despite the work involved, the joy of seeing your students learn and grow makes it all worthwhile.

Chapter 6: Step-by-step Guide to Creating Software Software: A Digital Powerhouse

In the world of digital products, software stands as a powerhouse with vast potential. The right piece of software can solve complex problems, enhance productivity, entertain, educate, and even transform industries. As we increasingly rely on digital technology in all facets of our lives, the demand for innovative and useful software continues to grow.

Whether it's a mobile app that helps users track their fitness goals, a project management tool that boosts team productivity, or a video game that offers an immersive experience, software creation presents an exciting avenue to make a significant impact and generate income.

Identifying a Software Need

The first step in creating a piece of software is to identify a need. This could be a problem that needs solving, a task that could be done more efficiently, or an entertainment gap that could be filled. Your own experiences and observations can be a good starting point. Market research, user surveys, and staying abreast of technological and industry trends can also provide insights into potential software needs.

Once you have identified a need, consider your target users. Who will benefit from your software? What are their characteristics, behaviors, and preferences? Understanding your target users will guide your software development process and help ensure your software meets their needs.

Planning Your Software

Once you've identified a need and understood your target users, the next step is to plan your software. This involves defining the functionality of your software – what it will do and how it will do it.

Start by identifying the key features your software needs to fulfill its purpose. Then, design the user flow - the steps a user will take to complete actions within your software.

Sketch out your initial ideas, creating rough wireframes of how your software will look and function. This initial planning phase helps to solidify your ideas and provides a blueprint for the development phase.

Developing Your Software

Software development is the process of bringing your plans to life. This involves coding your software, making it functional and interactive.

There are various programming languages and development frameworks you can use, depending on the type of software you're creating. You might be doing the development yourself, or you might be working with a team of developers.

As you develop your software, keep user experience at the forefront. Good software isn't just functional; it's also user-friendly. Ensure your software is intuitive to use, visually appealing, and provides clear feedback to user actions.

Remember, software development is often an iterative process. It involves testing, identifying bugs or issues, making improvements, and testing again. Patience and persistence are key.

Launching and Marketing Your Software

Once your software is developed and thoroughly tested, it's time to launch. This could involve making your software available on a platform like the Apple App Store or Google Play, or it might involve launching it on your own website.

Marketing is a critical step to get your software into the hands of users. Identify effective channels to reach your target users, and create a compelling message that highlights the benefits and features of your software. This could involve social media advertising, content marketing, email marketing, and more.

Conclusion

Creating a piece of software can be a complex and challenging journey, but it's also one of the most rewarding avenues in the realm of digital products. With every line of code, you're shaping a tool that can potentially make a significant impact on your users' lives or work. Be patient, be persistent, and remember why you embarked on this journey in the first place.

Chapter 7: Step-by-step Guide to Creating Digital Arts (Music, Design) The Artistic Side of the Digital World

Art has always been an essential aspect of human expression, and with the digital revolution, it has found new dimensions to unfold. Digital art, including music and design, has redefined artistic expression, expanded creative possibilities, and made art more accessible than ever before.

Whether it's a piece of digital music that moves hearts or a digital design that catches eyes, creating digital art allows you to express your creativity, connect with an audience worldwide, and generate income. This chapter will guide you through the process of creating digital music and design, two vibrant forms of digital art.

Creating Digital Music

Music has a unique way of reaching into our souls, and with digital technology, creating and sharing music has become more accessible. You don't need a recording studio to produce your music; a computer and the right software can give you a perfect start.

Identifying Your Musical Idea

Creating digital music starts with an idea. This could be a melody, a rhythm, a chord progression, or a lyrical concept. Capture your idea, however raw it might be, and use it as a foundation to build upon.

Creating Your Composition

With your idea in hand, you can start crafting your composition. Digital audio workstation (DAW) software, like Ableton Live, Logic Pro, or FL Studio, provides the tools you need to record, edit, mix, and arrange your music.

Start by laying down your basic idea, then build around it by adding more elements. This could involve creating drum patterns, playing synthesizer lines, or writing lyrics. DAWs provide a multitude of virtual instruments and effects, allowing you to experiment and create diverse sounds.

Mixing and Mastering Your Track

Once your composition is complete, the next stages are mixing and mastering. Mixing involves balancing the levels of your different tracks, applying effects, and ensuring all elements blend well together. Mastering is the final polish that optimizes your track for playback on all devices and systems.

Sharing Your Music

With your track mixed and mastered, you're ready to share it with the world. There are various platforms for publishing your music, like Spotify, Apple Music, and SoundCloud. You can also leverage social media platforms to promote your music and connect with your audience.

Creating Digital Design

Digital design encompasses a wide range of disciplines, including graphic design, web design, animation, and more. With the right software, you can create stunning visuals, express your creativity, and even make a living as a digital artist.

Identifying Your Design Concept

Similar to music, creating a digital design starts with a concept. What are you trying to communicate or express through your design? Sketch out your ideas, play with colors, shapes, and layouts, and develop a clear vision of what you want to create.

Creating Your Design

With your concept in hand, you can start creating your design using digital design software, l ike Adobe Photoshop or Illustrator. These tools provide an array of features that let you manipulate images, create vector graphics, adjust colors, apply effects, and more.

Take the time to learn and experiment with your chosen software. Mastering the tools and techniques can significantly enhance your design capabilities.

Finalizing and Sharing Your Design

Once you're happy with your design, it's time to finalize it. This may involve adding final touches, ensuring alignment and consistency, and exporting your design in the required format.

Sharing your design could involve uploading it to a portfolio website like Behance or Dribbble, using it as part of a client project, or selling it on a platform like Etsy or Redbubble.

Conclusion

Creating digital art, whether music or design, can be an enriching and fulfilling endeavor. It's a journey of self-expression, creativity, and connection. So, let your creativity flow, and immerse yourself in the incredible world of digital art.

Chapter 8: Step-by-step Guide to Creating Mobile Apps
Mobile Apps: The Digital Lifeline

The smartphone revolution has dramatically changed the way we live, work, and communicate, and at the heart of this revolution are mobile applications. From connecting with friends on social media apps, getting work done on productivity apps, to tracking health metrics on fitness apps, mobile applications have integrated seamlessly into our daily lives.

Creating a mobile app presents an opportunity to reach millions of smartphone users worldwide, offer valuable solutions, and generate income. Whether you're developing a simple tool or a complex platform, the process of creating a mobile app can be both challenging and rewarding.

Identifying the Need for Your App

Every successful mobile app starts with an idea, a concept that fulfills a specific need or solves a particular problem for its users. It's important to identify a unique value proposition that will make your app stand out in the crowded app marketplace.

To identify a need, you might consider your own experiences, conduct market research, or even involve potential users in discussions and surveys. Consider the pain points your target users face, and how your app can address those.

Planning Your App

With a clear idea in place, the next step is to plan your app. This involves defining what your app will do and how it will do it.

You'll need to think about the features your app will include, how users will navigate through the app, and what the user interface will look like. Sketch out your initial ideas and create wireframes, which are basic visual representations of your app's structure.

Designing Your App

Design is a crucial aspect of any mobile app. An app that is intuitive and appealing to use can greatly enhance user experience and engagement.

In designing your app, consider the principles of good mobile app design, such as simplicity, ease of use, consistency, and effective use of color and typography. Also, keep in mind the design guidelines for the specific platforms you're targeting, like iOS or Android.

Developing Your App

Once your plans and designs are ready, it's time for the development phase. This involves coding your app to make it functional. Depending on your skill set and the complexity of your app, you might do this yourself, hire a developer, or use an app development platform.

There are different programming languages for app development, like Swift and Objective-C for iOS apps, and Java or Kotlin for Android apps. If you want your app to work on both platforms, you might consider cross-platform development tools like React Native or Flutter.

Testing Your App

After the development phase, you'll need to thoroughly test your app to ensure it functions as expected and to identify and fix any bugs. Testing should cover all features, screen sizes, orientations, and potential user interactions.

Launching and Marketing Your App

Once your app is polished and ready, you can submit it to app stores like the Apple App Store or Google Play Store. Each has its own guidelines and review process, so make sure to comply with their requirements.

But getting your app on the app store is only part of the journey. You'll also need to market your app to reach potential users. This could involve social media marketing, in-app advertising, search engine marketing, and more.

Conclusion

Creating a mobile app can be a complex process, but seeing your app live and in the hands of users can be immensely rewarding. Remember that success often comes not from being first, but from being the best. So, keep refining, keep iterating, and keep improving your app. The journey is challenging, but the destination is worth it.

Chapter 9: Testing Your Digital Product

Why Testing Matters

Creating a digital product is an intricate process that requires a great deal of planning, design, development, and most importantly, testing. No matter how well-thought-out and designed your product might be, without thorough testing, it is impossible to guarantee a successful reception by the end users.

Testing provides a safeguard against unanticipated issues and uncovers potential areas for improvement that might not be immediately apparent. It offers a crucial perspective - the user's view. Regardless of the type of digital product, whether it's an app, software, eB ook, online course, or digital art, this user-centric view is essential in ensuring the product's real-world effectiveness and appeal.

Usability Testing: The User Perspective

Usability testing is a technique used in user-centered design to evaluate a product by testing it on users. It is one of the most effective methods of testing a digital product, as it provides

direct insight into how users interact with your product and where they may encounter difficulties.

Conducting usability testing involves several steps. First, you need to identify your target user base and recruit representative users for testing. Next, create specific tasks that these users will try to complete using your product.

As your test users engage with your product, observe their interactions carefully. Take note of any areas where they encounter difficulties or seem confused. Record both what they do and what they say, as their verbal feedback can offer additional insight into their experience.

Interpreting Feedback: The Art of Listening

The data gathered from usability testing can come in various forms, such as observed user behaviors, verbal comments, and performance on task completion. Interpreting this feedback involves identifying patterns, understanding the root causes of observed issues, and translating these insights into actionable improvements.

To effectively interpret feedback, it's essential to be both open-minded and objective. While some feedback may be easy to accept, other feedback might challenge your assumptions about the product. The key is to view all feedback as an opportunity for learning and improvement.

When analyzing feedback, look beyond the surface-level issues. For instance, if users struggled to complete a certain task, delve deeper into why they struggled. Was the interface unclear?

Were the instructions insufficient? Understanding the 'why' behind the feedback will guide you towards meaningful improvements.

From Feedback to Improvements: The Revision Process
Feedback is a catalyst for change. It highlights the areas of your product that need revision and points the way towards improvements.

Revising your digital product might involve a range of activities, from small design tweaks to major functionality updates. This is where the insights gained from feedback interpretation come into play. They inform your decisions about what changes to make and how to implement them.

Remember, the goal of revisions is not merely to fix problems, but to enhance the overall user experience. For instance, addressing a navigation issue might not just involve making the existing navigation clearer, but rethinking the navigation design to make it more intuitive.

Once revisions are made, the product should undergo another round of testing to ensure the changes have been effective and haven't introduced new issues. This cycle of testing, feedback, and revisions continues until the product achieves the desired level of quality and user satisfaction.

Conclusion

Testing is a vital part of the digital product creation process. It bridges the gap between the product's intended design and its real-world use. By conducting thorough usability testing, interpreting feedback effectively, and making informed revisions, you can ensure your product not only meets, but exceeds user expectations. The result is a digital product that is truly attuned to its users' needs, ready to make its mark in the digital landscape.

Chapter 10: Preparing for Launch

Laying The Foundation: Your Launch Plan

In the world of digital products, the launch is not a solitary event; it is an orchestrated culmination of various steps all converging into one pivotal moment. A well-crafted launch plan is your roadmap to this moment, outlining the strategies, tasks, and timelines leading up to the public availability of your digital product.

Crafting a launch plan requires a deep understanding of your product, its unique selling propositions, and the target audience. It involves identifying key milestones, such as when the product will be ready for testing, when promotional activities will begin, and when the product will go live. Remember, a good plan is both flexible and detailed, allowing you to adapt to unforeseen challenges while keeping sight of your overall objectives.

Establishing Your Online Presence: The Landing Page

In the digital world, a landing page is your product's storefront. It's the first impression potential users will have of your product, making it a critical component of your pre-launch strategy.

A successful landing page does more than just provide information about your product. It captures the attention of visitors, generates interest, and motivates them to take action, whether that's signing up for updates, pre-ordering the product, or sharing the page with others.

Designing an effective landing page involves balancing aesthetic appeal with functionality. The layout should be clean and intuitive, making it easy for visitors to navigate and understand your product's offerings. Pair this with compelling copy that highlights the benefits and unique features of your product, and you're on your way to creating a landing page that converts visitors into potential customers.

Igniting Interest: Pre-Launch Marketing Strategies Before your digital product sees the light of day, a buzz should already be brewing. Pre-launch marketing is all about building anticipation and creating a sense of excitement around your product. This early engagement can help to generate initial sales momentum and establish a user base even before the product launch.

Pre-launch marketing can take many forms, including email marketing campaigns, social media promotions, content marketing, and influencer partnerships. The key is to understand where your target audience spends their time and what type of content they engage with. Leveraging these insights can help you craft a pre-launch marketing strategy that resonates with your audience and builds anticipation for your product launch.

Setting the Right Price: Pricing Strategies

Pricing is a powerful tool that can influence the perceived value of your product, impact user behavior, and ultimately, drive your product's revenue and profitability. Determining the right price for your digital product requires a careful evaluation of several factors, including the cost of production, the perceived value of your product, competitor pricing, and your target audience's willingness to pay.

There are several pricing strategies you can consider. For example, a penetration pricing strategy involves setting a low initial price to attract users and gain market share, while a premium pricing strategy involves setting a high price to convey the superior quality or unique features of your product.

Remember, pricing is not a one-time decision but an ongoing process that may require adjustments based on user feedback, market trends, and your business objectives.

Conclusion

Preparing for the launch of a digital product is a multi-faceted process that sets the stage for your product's entrance into the market. From crafting a detailed launch plan to designing an engaging landing page, implementing effective pre-launch marketing strategies, and determining a competitive pricing strategy, each step is a piece of the puzzle that, when put together, can pave the way for a successful product launch. So, plan carefully, execute diligently, and anticipate the excitement of the launch with the confidence of thorough preparation.

Chapter 11: Selling Digital Products

Exploring the Marketplace: Selling Platforms

The digital realm is abundant with platforms designed to facilitate the sale of digital products, each offering its own unique features and benefits. Ranging from eCommerce giants like Amazon and eBay to digital-specific marketplaces such as Gumroad, Sellfy, or Shopify, these platforms cater to a wide array of digital products including eBooks, online courses, software, digital arts, and mobile apps.

Selecting the appropriate platform for your digital product entails a careful analysis of several factors, including the platform's user base, its compatibility with your product type, the cost of listing and selling, and its marketing and analytics capabilities. Each platform comes with its own unique audience and operational framework, making it vital to choose one that aligns with your product and business goals.

Social Media: A Sales Powerhouse

In today's interconnected world, social media isn't just a platform for sharing personal moments and trending memes; it's a powerful sales tool. Platforms like Facebook, Instagram, LinkedIn, and Twitter offer access to millions of potential customers, along with the tools to target them with precision.

Leveraging social media for sales involves more than just posting about your product. It's about engaging with your audience, understanding their needs and interests, and providing content that both entertains and informs. Social media advertising allows you to showcase your product to a highly targeted audience, while analytics tools offer insights into the performance of your posts and campaigns, helping you refine your strategy and boost your sales.

Email Marketing and SEO: The Art of Attraction

Two of the most effective methods to draw in potential customers are email marketing and Search Engine Optimization (SEO).

Email marketing allows you to directly communicate with individuals who have expressed an interest in your product or business. It's a chance to foster relationships, build customer loyalty, and promote your product in a personalized manner. Successful email marketing requires crafting compelling messages, segmenting your audience for more personalized communication, and analyzing engagement metrics to continuously improve your strategy.

Meanwhile, SEO is the practice of optimizing your website or landing page to rank higher in search engine results. Given that the majority of online experiences start with a search engine, implementing effective SEO practices can significantly increase your product's visibility, thereby boosting the chances of attracting and converting potential customers.

Extending Your Reach: Affiliate Marketing and Partnerships
Affiliate marketing and partnerships offer a way to extend your sales efforts beyond your immediate capabilities. In affiliate marketing, individuals or businesses promote your product to their audience, earning a commission for each sale they facilitate. This performance-based approach can significantly expand your product's reach, introducing it to audiences you might not have access to otherwise.

Partnerships, on the other hand, involve a mutual agreement between two businesses to promote each other's products. These can be particularly effective if the partner business shares a similar target audience but isn't a direct competitor.

Conclusion

Selling digital products successfully requires a well-rounded strategy that combines the power of various platforms, tools, and techniques. From choosing the right selling platform to harnessing the potential of social media, email marketing, SEO, and affiliate partnerships, each element plays a crucial role in capturing your audience's attention and converting their interest

into sales. Therefore, understanding and effectively implementing these components can set your digital product on the path to commercial success.

Chapter 12: Customer Support and Relationship Building The Heart of Your Business: Customer Support

In the realm of digital products, customer support isn't merely a function; it is a crucial pillar that upholds your business. As with any product or service, customers will inevitably encounter questions, concerns, or issues. In these instances, it's your customer support team that steps in, acting as the face of your business and the primary point of contact for your customers.

The importance of customer support in the digital product business cannot be overstated. It impacts everything from customer satisfaction and retention to your product's reputation and overall success. Effective customer support can turn a customer's negative experience into a positive one, reaffirming their trust in your product and fostering loyalty.

But customer support goes beyond merely addressing issues. It also involves educating customers about your product, helping them to get the most value from it, and continuously improving the user experience based on their feedback.

The Art of Excellent Customer Support

Delivering excellent customer support in the digital world requires a mix of responsiveness, empathy, patience, and expertise. It's about listening to your customers, understanding their needs and concerns, and providing effective solutions in a timely and respectful manner.

Excellent customer support begins with accessibility. Customers need to know that help is available when they need it, whether through email, live chat, phone, or even social media. It's important to provide multiple channels of communication and to ensure they're staffed by knowledgeable, well-trained support personnel.

Next, responsiveness is key. Quick, helpful responses show your customers that you value their time and are committed to resolving their issues. This doesn't mean rushing through interactions, but rather efficiently guiding customers to a resolution while making sure they feel heard and supported.

Finally, customer support should also focus on education. This involves providing resources such as guides, tutorials, FAQs, and forums where customers can learn more about your product, troubleshoot issues themselves, and connect with other users.

Fostering Long-Term Relationships with Customers

Customer support is just the starting point of building relationships with your customers.

Forging long-term relationships involves understanding your customers on a deeper level –

their needs, preferences, behaviors – and leveraging these insights to provide personalized experiences, communications, and offerings.

Effective communication plays a vital role in relationship building. This could mean sending regular newsletters with product updates and tips, offering personalized product recommendations, or simply checking in to ask for feedback. The goal is to engage with your customers in a meaningful way, showing them that you value their input and are committed to their satisfaction.

Loyalty programs are another effective tool for fostering long-term relationships. By rewarding customers for their continued patronage, you not only incentivize repeat purchases but also make your customers feel appreciated, enhancing their emotional connection to your product.

Handling Refunds and Complaints

Even with the most effective customer support, refunds and complaints are an inevitable part of doing business. How you handle these situations can significantly influence customer perceptions and the overall reputation of your product.

When dealing with refunds, it's important to have a clear, fair policy in place and to communicate it clearly to your customers. Handling refund requests should be a straightforward process, aiming to minimize inconvenience to the customer while protecting your business interests.

As for complaints, view them as an opportunity for learning and improvement rather than as a threat. Approach every complaint with an open mind, a willingness to understand the customer's perspective, and a commitment to resolving the issue to their satisfaction. A well-handled complaint can turn a disgruntled customer into a loyal advocate, while also providing valuable insights into potential areas of improvement for your product.

Conclusion

In the digital product business, customer support and relationship building are at the heart of long-term success. They form the basis of your interaction with your customers, influencing how they perceive, use, and value your product. By providing excellent customer support, fostering long-term relationships, and handling refunds and complaints effectively, you can create a loyal customer base, enhance the reputation of your product, and ultimately drive the growth and success of your business.

Chapter 12: Customer Support and Relationship Building The Heart of Your Business: Customer Support

In the realm of digital products, customer support isn't merely a function; it is a crucial pillar that upholds your business. As with any product or service, customers will inevitably encounter questions, concerns, or issues. In these instances, it's your customer support team that steps in, acting as the face of your business and the primary point of contact for your customers.

The importance of customer support in the digital product business cannot be overstated. It impacts everything from customer satisfaction and retention to your product's reputation and overall success. Effective customer support can turn a customer's negative experience into a positive one, reaffirming their trust in your product and fostering loyalty.

But customer support goes beyond merely addressing issues. It also involves educating customers about your product, helping them to get the most value from it, and continuously improving the user experience based on their feedback.

The Art of Excellent Customer Support

Delivering excellent customer support in the digital world requires a mix of responsiveness, empathy, patience, and expertise. It's about listening to your customers, understanding their needs and concerns, and providing effective solutions in a timely and respectful manner.

Excellent customer support begins with accessibility. Customers need to know that help is available when they need it, whether through email, live chat, phone, or even social media. It's important to provide multiple channels of communication and to ensure they're staffed by knowledgeable, well-trained support personnel.

Next, responsiveness is key. Quick, helpful responses show your customers that you value their time and are committed to resolving their issues. This doesn't mean rushing through interactions, but rather efficiently guiding customers to a resolution while making sure they feel heard and supported.

Finally, customer support should also focus on education. This involves providing resources such as guides, tutorials, FAQs, and forums where customers can learn more about your product, troubleshoot issues themselves, and connect with other users.

Fostering Long-Term Relationships with Customers

Customer support is just the starting point of building relationships with your customers.

Forging long-term relationships involves understanding your customers on a deeper level –

their needs, preferences, behaviors – and leveraging these insights to provide personalized experiences, communications, and offerings.

Effective communication plays a vital role in relationship building. This could mean sending regular newsletters with product updates and tips, offering personalized product recommendations, or simply checking in to ask for feedback. The goal is to engage with your customers in a meaningful way, showing them that you value their input and are committed to their satisfaction.

Loyalty programs are another effective tool for fostering long-term relationships. By rewarding customers for their continued patronage, you not only incentivize repeat purchases but also make your customers feel appreciated, enhancing their emotional connection to your product.

Handling Refunds and Complaints

Even with the most effective customer support, refunds and complaints are an inevitable part of doing business. How you handle these situations can significantly influence customer perceptions and the overall reputation of your product.

When dealing with refunds, it's important to have a clear, fair policy in place and to communicate it clearly to your customers. Handling refund requests should be a straightforward process, aiming to minimize inconvenience to the customer while protecting your business interests.

As for complaints, view them as an opportunity for learning and improvement rather than as a threat. Approach every complaint with an open mind, a willingness to understand the customer's perspective, and a commitment to resolving the issue to their satisfaction. A well -

handled complaint can turn a disgruntled customer into a loyal advocate, while also providing valuable insights into potential areas of improvement for your product.

Conclusion

In the digital product business, customer support and relationship building are at the heart of long-term success. They form the basis of your interaction with your customers, influencing how they perceive, use, and value your product. By providing excellent customer support, fostering long-term relationships, and handling refunds and complaints effectively, you can create a loyal customer base, enhance the reputation of your product, and ultimately drive the growth and success of your busines

Chapter 14: Conclusion

Beyond the Horizon: Future Trends in Digital Products As we stand on the brink of another wave of digital transformation, it's an exhilarating time to be involved in the creation and sale of digital products. Technologies such as artificial intelligence, virtual and augmented reality, blockchain, and the Internet of Things are rapidly evolving, bringing about new possibilities for digital product innovation.

The future is likely to see a growing convergence of physical and digital realms, with digital products playing an integral role in almost every aspect of our lives. At the same time, as technology continues to democratize access to digital product creation and distribution, competition in the digital space is likely to intensify. Staying ahead will require a keen eye on emerging trends, a relentless focus on customer needs, and a willingness to innovate.

Staying Agile: Continual Learning and Adapting

In the dynamic landscape of digital products, learning and adaptation are not just beneficial; they are essential. The rapid pace of technological change means that what worked today may not work tomorrow. Success in this realm requires staying updated with the latest tools, techniques, and best practices, and being ready to adapt your strategies and offerings accordingly.

Continuous learning extends to understanding your customers as well. As their needs and preferences evolve, so too should your digital products. Customer feedback, market research, and data analysis should be ongoing activities, providing you with the insights needed to keep your products relevant and competitive.

Final Words of Encouragement

As you embark or continue on your journey in the world of digital products, remember this: every successful product started as an idea. It was the result of someone's creativity, courage, and persistence. It faced challenges and setbacks, but through continuous learning, adaptation, and effort, it eventually found its place in the market.

Creating and selling digital products is not an easy journey, but it's one filled with immense potential and rewards. It provides an opportunity to transform your ideas into tangible products that can reach people around the world, impact their lives, and in the process, build a sustainable business.

So, as you go forth, be bold in your ideation, meticulous in your execution, and resilient in the face of challenges. Believe in your ideas, value your customers, and never stop learning and growing. Remember, every step you take in this journey brings you one step closer to your goal.

Here's to your success in the exciting world of digital products!

www.ingramcontent.com/pod-product-compliance
Lightning Source LLC
Chambersburg PA
CBHW072238230526

45466CB00025B/2113